Revolutionizing How to Love

A Guide to a Successful Relationship

Revolutionizing How to Love

A Guide to a Successful Relationship

Frank C. Johnson

Printed in the United States.

Published by Frank C. Johnson 8/2/2018
Revolutionizing How to Love
www.frankcjohnson.com

ISBN-13: 978-1724741240
ISBN-10: 1724741241

Dedication

It would only be fitting for me dedicate this book to my very first love, my mother, Genevieve. Ma, I dedicate this book to you, because you have consistently been the example of unconditional love, sacrifice and encouragement, and it is because of you I have been able to write a book regarding this raw emotion of love. You are the very first person to whom I uttered the most powerful 3 words one can say to another – "I love you". Intentionally or not, you have shown me how to pass this gift of love onto others, and equally as important, how to receive it. It is because of you that I can humbly say I am a great man. A man who has learned the importance of balancing both strength and sensitivity and can unapologetically embrace both of these qualities. A son always wants to make his momma proud and if I have been successful at doing so, just know I am a reflection of you. Love is too weak to define how much you mean to me, and I am eternally grateful to and for you. I love you!

Contents

Acknowledgement

I would like to acknowledge and thank my son, Franklin C. Johnson, Jr., sister, Kelly Johnson Severin, granddaughter, Leilani Johnson, best friend Nicole Brown and my godchildren, Khamden and Grayson Courtney for all of their continued support. Thank you for your encouragement and for never doubting anything I said I was going to accomplish. Whenever I am in need, I call and you all are there. For that I am grateful and I love you all.

Jessica Swindell. There aren't too many people in this world like you. You are selfless and genuine and you always encourage me to go after any goal I place in front of me. The completion of this book is greatly due to your unwavering support and words cannot express how thankful I am to call you one of my best friends! I love you.

Kaneen Morgan. I want to thank you so much for being there for me throughout this journey. You have spent countless hours on the phone with me, listening, guiding and encouraging me. You have believed in me and my message from the beginning and I thank you for that. Although we were introduced through a professional space, I am glad that we have graduated to becoming good friends. Thank you for holding my hand through this process. You are a gem.

Preface

Who This Book is For

At the time I began penning this book, I had been single for a little over seven years. Once it became known to my friends and family that I was writing a book on why relationships fail, the common question I received was, "What makes you so qualified to write a book about relationships?" My answer was consistent and simple, "I am living the example of how I believe relationships should be pursued and endured." You see, I believe we have been unintentionally hoodwinked, bamboozled and misguided when it comes to long-term love and relationships. We have been following a generational system, which thus far has been unsuccessful.

My objective is to completely revolutionize the way relationships are sought, and what we should do once we recognize we aren't being truly fulfilled by our spouse or significant other. My hope is to drastically decrease the number of failed relationships and marriages we have today and to see a significant increase in happy, functional and monogamous relationships. Happiness should be the norm when romantically involved with someone and not an unusual or chaotic circumstance. Unfortunately, it is so much easier to find couples who are enduring unhappy relationships than it is to find couples who are genuinely happy with the ones they've CHOSEN to be with.

I understand new concepts can initially be difficult to grasp, but I ask that you take this journey with me and maintain an open mind to change. If we all want to have a greater chance for a successful relationship then we inevitably need to do things much differently. If we don't, then we will continue to receive the same unsuccessful results. I believe I can help you and so many others recognize and enjoy the beauty of a happy, functional monogamous relationship, which is what we all strive to have.

This book was written for anyone, male or female, who is absolutely ready to be in a relationship with someone. I am writing for those who are tired of the same old, same old, and for anyone who is ready to do the very necessary, and oftentimes difficult ground work, in order to achieve good, TRUE love.

Change can be difficult, but if you are willing and determined to go through the rough patches when they arise, in order to achieve your goal of a loving relationship, then this book is for you. You will certainly need to change your mind-set to undo the way things have been unsuccessfully done in the past and allow yourself the opportunity to go down a road you have never traveled before. Admittedly, at times this ride may be bumpy and uncomfortable, but I am confident you will reach your desired destination, if you're able to stay on this course. This journey will require you to be completely honest with yourself, and about yourself, in order for this to work. Denial must be a thing of the past! If you know that living in the land of denial is where you are most comfortable, and you aren't quite ready to let go of it, reading this book will not be beneficial to you. Personal growth requires truth and sometimes the truth is difficult to handle, but you must remember that you possess the power to handle it.

Most of us are aware of the faults and shortcomings we have. These are the things that have prohibited us from maintaining a functional relationship, and it's no longer satisfactory to expect others to accept you with these "faults" or very challenging aspects of your personality, when you have the capability of improving them. For example: If you know that your anger management needs to improve in order to have a more peaceful and harmonious relationship, then you should accept the responsibility of changing it for the better. If your unwarranted jealousy issues are preventing you and your spouse from progressing as a couple, it is incumbent upon you to find out why you have these issues. Expecting your spouse to accept the unacceptable does nothing but continue the dysfunction you're expecting to get rid of.

"Loving you as you are" is one of many misguided ideologies handed down to us, and too many of us have accepted this way as to "how it should be." It's wrong!

Don't you want to receive the best version of the person you want to spend the rest of your life with? Why wouldn't you want to give that same person the best version of yourself? This isn't about becoming a perfect person as much as it is about realizing that perhaps there are things about ourselves, or our personalities, we must change/improve, if we realistically expect to be in a happy relationship. I will be making reference to being "happy, functional and monogamous" several times throughout this book, because I want to keep the objective in the forefront of your mind. If you are reading this book, then being happy, functional and monogamous should be one of your objectives. So, my redundancy is intentional, simply to remind you of your goal and to ensure that you stay focused and on track.

Denial is a place of comfort and is so detrimental to you and your relationships. What really sucks is that you CHOOSE to be there.

You and I will be doing something anomalous, as it pertains to figuring out why relationships fail. There are many books out there outlining various reasons as to why they fail, but we will be doing it a bit differently. Other books provide a plethora of examples of the do's and don'ts if you desire to have a successful relationship. For instance, they suggest for people to openly communicate, and that they shouldn't cheat or abuse their spouse. All of these things, plus many others are very true, but they are also the obvious reasons for turmoil or breakups.

Partaking in any of these activities, while in a committed relationship, will certainly prevent you from achieving the type of relationship we all seek; yet still it's done every single day by people who claim to love the ones they are doing them to. This book will take you beneath the surface of the obvious flaws and typical reasons why relationships fail. We will delve into why you may have insecurities, anger issues, or the propensity to cheat and/or constantly lie to the one you expect to trust you. I'm sure at this point in your life you are aware of, or have been made aware of, the flaws you may have, which contribute or may have contributed to your failing or failed relationships.

Knowing or realizing their existence is only half of the battle. It's also about owning and fixing them to ensure that you don't repeat the same situations over and over again. This may prove to be challenging for some, perhaps even most, but I hope you can put trust into this process and fight to become a better you, whenever you feel yourself being resistant, if and when the process becomes difficult.

Sometimes we have to go through some bad in order to get to some good. You know what I mean? As an example, drinking cod liver oil isn't the most pleasant experience, but after we pinch our noses, commit to drinking it, and make all the ugly faces we need to make to ensure we don't bring it back up, our bodies will begin to reap the many benefits that cod liver oil has to offer. With that being said, I am excited and very confident this book will do the same for you. Let's get started!

Chapter 1

The Genesis of Love for Me

True, healthy love is an emotion we all innately desire. So many of us spend our lifetime in search of this intangible, yet omnipresent thing, which governs so many aspects of our lives. From the time of our birth, we crave a connection from our mothers and fathers and continue to search for that special someone we hope will be by our side until the very end of our lives.

From fairy-tale storybooks and cinema to our parents, it is expected that we will meet our soul mates at a young age, get married, have children and live happily ever after. And, in order for this fairy-tale to have a happy ending, this union will require a lot of hard work. I don't believe this to be necessarily true, and I will show you how this ideology has unfortunately become the norm for most couples.

For as long as I can remember, I have always been a lover of love. As a child, I can vividly remember receiving lots of love and affection from my mother and older sister. For some reason, I recognized very early on in life that true love is always healthy and it feels good. If it doesn't provide you with a euphoric feeling, then all you really have is an imposter, posing as love. In retrospect, I believe the love I've experienced as a child was the genesis of me understanding the importance of cherishing and spreading this raw emotion.

I was born on the beautiful island of St. Thomas, located in the United States Virgin Islands, and I moved to New York when I was 3 months old with my mother and 20-month-old sister, Vonda-kay. My mother and father was a young, married couple, and the plan was for him to go to the U.S. ahead of us to get things settled and then send for us to join him. Unfortunately, or fortunately, the plan didn't come together as my mother anticipated.

While setting up shop, my father wound up creating a life and lifestyle of his own, which didn't include his wife or his children. So, my mother suddenly found herself to be a single parent and the sole provider for two small children, in a foreign country without family or friends or any form of support. We now called home a two-bedroom apartment, nestled in an impoverished neighborhood in the "Boogie Down" Bronx section of New York City. As you can imagine, this would have been an extremely trying and stressful time for my mother, who was absolutely my superhero. She was able to wrap my sister and I up in her protective cape of love and shielded us from the difficulties and hardships she endured during this period of our lives. She somehow found a way to make the best of our circumstances and kept us safe in the environment we lived in. To this day, I can take a deep breath, close my eyes and reminisce on that time of my life and literally feel how loved I was as a child. That capability in itself is a blessing.

A couple of years later, my mother began dating someone pretty seriously, and I can remember my very first encounter with her boyfriend. At the tender age of 3, I can recall how much I didn't like him. I believe my spirit didn't take to his, and I could feel the negativity whenever I was in his presence. Obviously, I didn't realize what it was at the time, but as I regress, what else could it have been? They married when I was 5 years old and suddenly that was the beginning of the end of the tranquility and synergy I had known all of my young life.

My mother and new stepfather were the quintessential polar opposites. The cliché, "opposites attract" certainly was applicable in their relationship, which was consistently turbulent and dysfunctional. My mother was a vibrant, fun and loving person, who was adored by anyone who met her. On the other hand, my stepfather was a strict, militant, anti-social recluse, sprinkled with a touch of dominance in his personality. Okay, okay! It was a bit more than just a touch. It was his way or the highway, which would lead to a serious problem if he was ever met with opposition. From the first day we were introduced, I knew there would never come a time when my feelings of dislike toward him would ever change for the better. That dislike quickly graduated to, "I can't stand him," which seamlessly morphed into inevitable hate.

Despite how bad of a relationship I had with my stepfather, my mother was still tightly bonded with me and my sister. In fact, I believe our bond had become even stronger. Perhaps it was because she inevitably felt the negative energy he brought to the home, so she showered us with even more love and affection, with the hopes of combating the off-putting vibes he brought.

Over the years, although I had received plenty of love from my mother, it wasn't enough to eradicate the anger I had developed from having a man in my life I didn't like, and whose blood I didn't share, possessing so much authority over me, my mother and sister. I hated it with every fiber of my being, and because I couldn't do anything about it, rage and anger was my outlet. I didn't walk around with a snarl or intense creases in my forehead, but let's just say, I certainly developed a very short fuse. If anyone had spoken to me in a tone I didn't appreciate, I wouldn't hesitate to let them know how I felt about it. One can gauge the number of arguments my stepfather and I had by the amount of dents and craters my knuckles imprinted on my mother's refrigerator door. Punching the refrigerator was better than punching another person, and I was also aware that it had a lot more give than the walls did. I was no dummy.

As I transitioned into becoming a teenager, and after my mother upgraded her refrigerator to one with a much more resilient surface, the relationship did not improve between my stepfather and the rest of the family. Yet, five years after being married, my mother gave birth to my first little sister, Katherine. Four years after Katherine's birth, Kelly was welcomed into this world. Children are often seen as blessings, but when a family was as dysfunctional as ours, these two births actually caused more of a wedge between my parents than did any semblance of closeness, never mind displaying a tinge of functional love.

Abuse comes in many forms. There's physical abuse, mental abuse, sexual abuse and emotional abuse. There are also varying degrees of these abuses, yet they are all horrific and traumatizing in their own right. My stepfather was an officer in the Korean War, and so we were more like his little soldiers than we were little children. He certainly wasn't opposed to corporal punishment and many of the "lessons" we were being taught would be grounds for an arrest these days. Although these beating weren't daily or even weekly, when they did happen, they were intense. We were usually beaten with a belt, which often felt like an eternity. Again, that's where my anger began to fester. I was just a child, unable to physically defend myself or my sister from a person I never considered to be my father from beating her or I for doing things within the normal realm of what children do. I used to tell myself after being taught a "lesson" that once I turned 16, he was no longer going to be able to punish, beat or even discipline me ever again. I vowed those days would be forever gone! Whelp, I've always been quite the goal achiever, and I reached it at the age of 13!

Early one Saturday morning, he woke me to discuss something trivial, which certainly could have waited until I had gotten up naturally on my own. He began his usual interrogation and speech, which soon escalated to one of our usual arguments. This one had a lot more heat and venom behind it, which led into our very first physical fight. Yes, a fight! Over the years, we had plenty of physical altercations, except I was the only recipient of the blows, and I never extended any of my own. But, today was going to be a new day, one neither of us would ever forget.

I was tired of being bullied, beaten and punished for ridiculous reasons like this one, so I decided to finally stand up for myself and fight back. Me, lashing back at him physically was more impulsive, as my anger was in control of my actions. He was a grown man, and I was just a scrawny, scrappy kid, but this time I was empowered and weaponized with pent-up anger and resentment, which gave me the physical strength equal to a man. He was shocked at me fighting back, but he was even more shocked at how I was no longer the victim, I was now the dominator. He was unable to control me in this fight, as we tussled, overturned tables and chairs, and I was completely done with him having the upper hand. This was my declaration of manhood, and I stated it with an exclamation point and explicit verbal dares for him to ever try and put his hands on me again. After my mother separated us, he got dressed, left the house and came back several hours later. I learned later that evening, he had spent most of the day at the emergency room treating a strained neck. I realized at that very moment that there are only three ways for an individual to be controlled by another:

1) **Mentally.** If you can control someone's mind, you can control his or her actions. You can convince them to do things you want them to do, regardless of how they feel about doing it.

2) **Financially.** To live in a society where money is a necessity and if you aren't generating enough income of your own to be self-sufficient, it can be a detrimental situation if you are dependent upon someone who will exploit and abuse your dependence on them.

3) **Physically.** If you can physically dominate someone, you can oftentimes make him or her acquiesce to your demands, for their fear of being physically harmed for resisting.

There was never a point where he was able to control me mentally, and my mother was there to cover me financially, but I was afraid of the physical beatings and control that I believed he had over me. Once I realized and unleashed my underestimated physical strength, I knew he could no longer physically control me. That day I took my independence and embraced my new freedom!

Realizing your potential is a liberating feeling, which can give you the wings you need to fly and excel. I stripped the bully of his "power" over me and it felt great. Admittedly, once I took back my power I would flaunt it, because essentially I knew there was nothing he could do about it. I realized my power, my worth and my rights, plus the inner strength that I now had to ensure they were honored and respected.

We still resided in the same dysfunctional household, so it was only a matter of time before we had gotten into another big physical fight, which was about two years after the first one. Perhaps he thought me dominating him the first time was a fluke, as this altercation was worse than the first for him. I was 2 years older, stronger, plus I had even more resentment and dislike for him. Again, he had to visit the emergency room for an even more serious injury than the first time we fought. The "lesson" he learned was to never, ever attempt to teach me anything else again. He was a quick study, as he never did.

There was NEVER a point when we were a happy family. How can happiness be possible, when you have someone so profoundly dysfunctional in your immediate circle, constantly spewing toxic energy? It's an impossibility that so many try to make a reality, and they fail terribly each time. If you have a cup of clear water and mix it with another cup of water laced with cyanide, and you pour them both into a bowl, that clear water will absolutely become poisoned or "toxic." The only way for the clear water to remain clear is if whatever it's mixed with is also clear. The same concept applies to relationships. Having just one person who is dysfunctional is enough to dominate and destroy whatever positivity the relationship has to offer. The dysfunction will contaminate the relationship, guaranteed.

Ultimately, my mother and stepfather divorced, but not before the psychological damage had been done to everyone who lived amid the profound dysfunction we all endured over the years. None of us were left emotionally unscathed. I was fortunate to recognize very early on that I needed emotional and psychological repair, and so my journey to do so began.

Chapter 2

Acceptance of the Ugly Beautifies You

Most of us are unfortunately, or fortunately, depending on our philosophy about "life," were born and or raised into homes filled with different forms and levels of dysfunction. Whether it was experienced directly or indirectly, abuse of alcohol, drugs, emotional or physical abuse, sexual improprieties, abandonment, etc.—all of these tragic issues have shaped us in ways that inevitably coexists with varying degrees of pain, which are usually accompanied with unfavorable, self-sabotaging behaviors. As children, we soak up these taught behaviors like sponges. If we don't recognize and repair the emotional and psychological damage caused by these terrible "lessons," there is a great probability of gravitating toward these same behaviors, which had caused the pain and horrible memories stemmed from our childhood.

It's ironic and puzzlingly true. These behaviors can be cyclical and generational, as you will teach your children what you've been taught as a child, both the good and bad. The cycle will continue to spread like a virus until a valiant effort is made to break it. Victims of abuse often become abusers themselves, recycling the same hurt and dysfunctional behaviors they've experienced. Addressing one's abuse must be met and dealt with in order for their negative behaviors to be changed for the better. Simply put, you can't heal what you won't reveal. Revisiting any traumatic experience will require a great deal of courage, but acceptance of the trauma is where the strength lies to free you from its bondage and control.

Facing Yourself

As previously stated, I grew up in a very dysfunctional household and the way I dealt with my learned behaviors was through anger. People used to ask me regularly, "Why are you so angry?" And of course, I used to get angry whenever I was asked that question. It was frustrating, because I didn't understand what they were talking about, as I was unaware of my anger issues. I knew I had the propensity to argue a point to the ground, but I saw those conversations as healthy debates. The fact is that there was nothing healthy about them, as they were just plain old arguments. Finally, I had an epiphany and realized that everyone else couldn't be wrong, and I felt it was time for me take a closer look at myself. Whenever we look in the mirror, there is always the possibility of not liking something we see. This is why we spend so much

11

time looking at everyone else, rather than focusing on what's right in front of us. So, let's all focus!

The time for me to address the man in the mirror was long overdue. Denial is the blinder we wear through life as we try to convince ourselves that we aren't the problem, while pointing our fingers at everyone else. This is why honest self-reflection can be a challenge for so many people, but I knew I needed to remove my emotions and ego from the equation and look at the truth square in the eye. I soon recognized that they were right, and I was wrong. I was angry, short tempered, argumentative, and I wanted to do something about it. I wanted to make a change for the better, because I knew being this angry was not going to be a positive thing for me or anyone else around me—especially when I was ready to start a family of my own. I sincerely wanted to break the cycle, so I began the humbling journey of doing so.

Ironically, after spending the majority of my childhood praying to get away from my militant stepfather, three months after graduating high school, I enlisted into the United States Army. The military provided me with a clear understanding of accountability and the importance of building the strong mind-set needed to accomplish the tasks I set out to achieve. I was also taught how to control the anger that had been festering within me for almost 15 years. I was taught about making choices and their repercussions and the consequences of my actions, which were extremely instrumental in my learning how to control my anger. I was no longer impulsive, and I became much more calculating and aware of the cause and effect of my actions.

Living in the Realm of Truth

This was a very auspicious time for me in many ways and enlisting was certainly one of the best decisions I've ever made to date. Being under that umbrella of controlled discipline versus the chaotic, abusive discipline I was familiar with is where I began to read various genres of books, especially the soft covers located in the self-help section. They were terrific teachers that showed me how to get out of my own way and recognize my ego whenever it decided to rear its ugly head. I worked hard to live in the realm of true reality and not dwell in the space of the false reality I had created in my mind, which was occupied by only my wants and my ego. I was now cognizant of my anger and made it a point to suppress it when I felt it begin to roar. I learned that being upset or angry was literally a choice. We are emotional creatures, so feeling is part of our nature, but we should all be in total control of our emotional state at all times. The more this concept is practiced, the easier it becomes to implement.

We are all products of our environments and life experiences. Many times the genesis of our dysfunction can be traced back to the household we grew up in as children. Other times, traumatizing experiences later on in life can also be the cause of dysfunctional behaviors.

Regardless if they are good or bad, positive or negative, our experiences shape us in whichever way we allow them to. We absolutely have a choice in how these issues are addressed, and if these negative issues go unchecked, they usually manifest themselves in a hindering manner at some point in life.

For me, my outlet was anger. For others, it may be the excessive use of drugs, alcohol, overeating, gambling, promiscuity, living in false realities, or a host of other self-sabotaging ways. These are just a few of the coping mechanisms we create in order to deal with the roars of the subconscious demons we try so hard to keep silent. The truth is, we can spend the rest of our lives pretending they don't exist, but they will continue to be attached to you like a shadow until you choose to recognize their existence and do the work necessary to exorcise them out of your life forever.

Learn to Admit the Truth

The first step to fixing a problem is to admit there is one. Acknowledgement and acceptance is the key to self-development, and living in denial is the lock that inevitably stunts your growth and prevents you from being the best possible version of yourself. Both acknowledgement and denial are equally available options for you to choose from. Unfortunately, to their own detriment, most people tend to choose the latter. People find it to be much easier or more comfortable to create a world of denial, which suppresses the emotions and memories of their painful pasts. But, is living a life in denial really the easier choice? Absolutely not. It's actually much easier to truly ACCEPT your past as being a part of your reality and view these difficult experiences as hard life lessons you had to learn than it is to live your life manifesting dysfunctional behaviors that only rob you of the happiness you could be enjoying and sharing.

Acceptance and pro-action to remedying your situation is the path you need to take in order to be successful at bettering/healing yourself. I have a very good friend named Elizabeth who has struggled with being overweight her entire life. She has tried to lose weight on just about every popular diet advertised and even some that aren't. She has confided in me of the daily difficulties she faces, which are directly attributed to the excess weight she carries around with her 24 hours a day. She says she gets winded after walking up two flights of stairs and standing for long periods of time is hard on her knees and ankles. She lamented that sex can often be awkward and less enjoyable due to her insecurities about her body and her physical limitations due to her size. She would love to rectify all of these problems by losing the weight, but there is something inside of her that has proven to be much stronger than her will, which prevents her from successfully losing the weight. If she could snap her fingers and magically be at her ideal weight, she would, but she can't.

This is what I mean by living in reality and not the alternate realities we tend to create. I've watched her vigorously and enthusiastically start out many firsts of January with the determination needed to shed the excess weight she has spent her lifetime putting on. But, unfortunately, shortly after she begins this weight loss journey, she would revert back to her old bad habits, which casted her into the situation she so desperately wants to get out of.

Some people are able to "fix" themselves without the help of a therapist or a professional, but others need some kind of assistance. I've suggested therapy to her on many occasions and have explained how beneficial and life changing it could potentially be. After years of trying, I've only gotten resistance from her, as she claims that she "doesn't need therapy." That's her being in denial and living in her alternate reality. Similarly to how an alcoholic would say that he/she could stop drinking whenever they want to and don't need to go to Alcoholics Anonymous. She has also confided in me about the sexual abuse she has survived as a child, which I believe has contributed to her self-sabotaging behaviors. There are many other contributing factors that she has suppressed and she simply sees them as past experiences she has gotten over. The self-sabotaging behaviors she indulges in suggests otherwise.

Denial is the cancer that grows in far too many people, and the only cure for it is acknowledging the pain, acceptance of your trauma and CHOOSE to release it. You should have it embedded in your mind that denial is absolutely the greatest personal growth stunter and you can't improve the things you won't acknowledge need improvement.

A good therapist would help her address the sexual abuse she experienced and also the abandonment issues she has endured by her parents, and show her how she uses food as comfort to cope with the pain she has suppressed and continues to suppress. This is a classic example of someone who believes it to be easier to live with the pain they have tucked away deep down inside of themselves, than it is to face the pain of these bad experiences head-on.

Accepting any traumatic experience as a horrible truth of your past strips it of its power over you. This is where it is vulnerable and also where your window of opportunity lies to conquer it and free yourself from its bondage. Doing this will allow for growth and this newfound strength will allow you to really flourish. Unfortunately, because of her unwillingness to seek the help she obviously needs to overcome her plaguing demons, she continues to be overweight to this day, and she also continues to endure all of the difficulties that comes along with being overweight.

My second favorite English word, with love being the first, is the very profound and powerful word, acceptance.

Acceptance is often conflated with understanding or comprehension. One can understand the gravity of a situation or comprehend all of the elements of a circumstance they have no control over, without actually ACCEPTING the reality of said circumstance.

To illustrate my point, let's use two women with identical lives as an example. They are both of the same age, have the same level of education, and economic backgrounds. They are also in relationships with men, who are also identical in every way for the exact same period of time. They are equally devastated when they learn that they've been cheated on by their significant others, something both women deem intolerable, which consequently ends both of their relationships.

Woman #1 allows herself a set amount of time to come to terms with the transgression made against her and also allows her heart time to mourn the loss of this relationship, which she had such high hopes, for years. She understands the importance of being in tune with her feelings, while NOT allowing it to negatively impact her present and future happiness. After this designated time frame passes, she vows to move on to the next chapter of her life and accepts this life experience as one of the many lessons she is determined to learn.

Woman #2 takes a very different approach to handling her pain. She becomes angry, resentful, depressed and dependent upon whatever vices she has that bring her comfort during stressful times. She becomes reclusive, decides not to trust any more men and constantly seeks the answer to her question of "*Why.*"

Remember, these two women are identical in every facet, except for one thing. Woman #1 has the ability to ACCEPT her pain and situation as her reality and woman #2 hasn't been able to do the same. What most people don't realize is that we literally make a choice on how we feel about something and for how long. When you ALLOW something you have control over to occur in your life, it's something you've CHOSEN to do. Whether or not you are aware of this power, your ability to control your feelings exists within you. You can choose to control them or you can choose for them to control you, but either way, you are the one making the choice.

Both women had the option to accept their unfortunate situations, but only one did, and she allowed herself the opportunity to learn, move on and grow. The other chose to wallow in her depression and stunted her own growth by not accepting her difficult reality.

It's usually pretty easy to accept situations you are in favor of than those that may cause you pain or grief. For instance, it's much easier to accept being hired for a job position you have applied for than it is to be fired from a job you need and or enjoy. The two examples used above are interchangeable variables to showcase the concept of acceptance. Whether it's the loss of a love, job, or even a life, you get to choose how you're going to feel about your new reality and for how long.

Too many people falsely believe they are born with a certain temperament, and however they are is how they are destined to be. This mind-set will need to be completely revamped if you want to adopt the concept of acceptance. Revamped is the operative word. This concept of acceptance may be a little difficult for some to grasp at first, but with practice and a valiant effort, it too can be mastered. Once you have made this concept your ideology, you will be happier, calmer, less stressed and a much more patient person. You will be surprised at how much of your time is freed up, once you don't spend it worrying and stressing over situations you have no control over.

How does one develop the ability to accept situations that they would typically resist? The first thing is to admit having the propensity to resist situations that aren't in line with your level of comfort, wants or needs. Once that's accomplished, the next step is learning how to recognize when you are being resistant. The truest telling sign is the creation of "excuses" for tasks you could have accomplished. An excuse is nothing more than a self-indulged ego stroke, which prevents you from completing goals or tasks you are capable of accomplishing, due to you not doing what you SHOULD do versus you doing what you WANT to do.

We usually know what we need to do in order to be successful at whatever it is we are setting out to accomplish. Whether it's to lose a certain amount of weight, to learn a language or to save 10 percent of every paycheck. If your actions toward these goals are inconsistent with what's needed to successfully accomplish these goals, then you are creating excuses.

Recognizing when you're making excuses should be easy, because it's very difficult to believe a lie you tell yourself. Similarly, when you tell a lie to someone else, there is an internal trigger that alerts you of your dishonesty. If you were supposed to meet someone at 7:00 pm and you don't get there until 7:30 pm, because you wanted to finish watching an episode of your favorite TV show, don't blame your tardiness on traffic when you've reached your destination! You know inside exactly why you were late. There's an internal voice that tells you, "Now, you know that's not true!"

When you hear that voice, do not dismiss it. That's the trigger, which will help to keep you on track whenever you veer off of it. Recognize it, embrace it and allow it to have the power of keeping you honest with yourself and others. This is vital to becoming successful at adopting the concept of acceptance. You can apply this to whatever goal you've set out to accomplish.

We have all heard the saying, "practice makes perfect," and this philosophy certainly rings true when it comes to mastering the concept of acceptance. The objective is to positively change many facets of your life, including experiencing a healthy, loving and lasting relationship. To this day I am cognizant of my actions and reactions to situations, and I check myself regularly on when I'm making excuses, regardless of the task. Whether the variable is me going to the gym, putting in quality time to write this book or facing difficult issues head-on, stemmed from my childhood.

The concept is exactly the same for them all. Once you know what needs to be done to successfully complete the task, all you have to do is execute the action. One of my favorite slogans is, "Just do it" by Nike. As long as you have the capability of accomplishing your goal, then just do it. Don't procrastinate or conjure up excuses as to why you can't do the things you should be doing, regardless of how challenging the journey to completing your tasks may be.

You may not feel like going to the gym today or you may not feel like reliving your painful past in therapy, but if that's what it takes to be successful, then that's what you should be doing. Being successful is not about a "feeling," it's about doing what you need to do, whether you FEEL like doing it or not. The choice is truly yours to make.

Being the best possible version of yourself will establish a broad-based foundation that will support the happy, functional, monogamous relationship you are striving to have. And the person who will be in that relationship with you is doing, or has done, the same self-improving work you are doing. You wouldn't build your dream house on quicksand, would you? You would want to build it on a sturdy foundation to ensure support for this magnificent dream house of yours. In order for your dream relationship to not collapse or crumble, it also requires a sturdy foundation. This foundation is the combined, individual strength of you and your significant other. It will take the strength of you both to stay strong as a unit.

I tend to practice what I preach. I have explained in earlier chapters the difficulties I've experienced growing up in a dysfunctional household. But, not all traumatic experiences happens early in life. Sometimes horrible things happen to adults, and they have to find a way to cope with their new reality. For me it was being in an elevator accident, which subsequently resulted in very serious injuries to my neck, back, knee and ankle. I eventually needed to have an ankle surgery, knee surgery, 3 procedures on my spine and I still need to have a full knee replacement in a couple of years.

Prior to the accident, I was a very physical person. I worked out regularly, ran around Prospect Park, in Brooklyn a few times a week and played all sorts of sports. From basketball to martial arts, to H.I.I.T. (high intensity interval training). For as long as I have known myself, I have always been a very athletic person. I played on organized baseball and basketball teams in high school and was even talented enough to have boxed for the U.S. Army boxing team. But, once the accident happened, my physicality came to a screeching halt! This was a huge challenge for me to deal with physically and also mentally.

I remember discussing my upcoming ankle surgery with my doctor and him telling me that the surgery was going to be very difficult and I was going to be down for approximately six months to recover. I knew my surgery was scheduled for January and I immediately did the math and realized that according to him, I should be healed and ready to go around July. I vividly remember excitedly responding to him, "That's perfect! I will be able to start running again in July!" I will never forget the disappointing look he had when he said to me, "I'm sorry, but your running days are over."

I recall thinking to myself that he doesn't know me and my determined mind, and how I was going to prove him wrong! I did have the surgery in January and I must admit that he was correct, it was extremely difficult. The recovery was very painful, but I got through it by constantly reminding myself that this too shall pass. I fought through the frustration of being immobile for so long and not being able to be pain free. I counted down the months and couldn't wait for July to come, so I could defy my surgeon's prediction. Unfortunately, he was correct. Between my bummed knee and my ankle, running was and still is an impossibility.

As you can imagine, this was devastating to me. I went through a phase of depression, because I was no longer able to do so many things I had taken for granted. Simple things like standing up to wash dishes, bending over to tie my shoes or to even sit down for a long period of time. None of these things could be done any longer without some form of pain or discomfort being present. I had to face my new reality and find a way to cope with it. How did I cope with it? I accepted it! I can no longer run, so now I ride my bike. I cannot lift heavy weights like I used to anymore, so now I trick my body and use resistance bands, in a way to not put any stress on my lower back and neck. I adjusted to my reality. I reluctantly acknowledged my limitations, I accepted it as being beyond my control and I am moving on. Living my life as happily and as productively as I possibly can.

Refuse to allow circumstances to stunt your growth or enjoyment of life. You have one life to live, so live it happily and productively. Choose happiness.

My traumatic experience may be completely different than yours, but just how I refuse to allow my circumstance to stunt my growth or enjoyment of life, you have to find a way to do the same. We only have one life to live, so live it as happily and as productively as YOU possibly can.

I shared that story with you because I want you to understand I am no different than you are. We all have the ability to make a choice. You can choose to quit or to give up hope or you can choose to fight for the life you want to have and enjoy. I say, fight! Your life is worth it.

Chapter 3

Mend the Broken You

We know that dysfunctional behavior is real and is the cancer to all relationships, intimate or otherwise. Dysfunction typically exacerbates itself, unless a conscious effort is made to get rid of it. The logic is actually very simple, which is, you get what you have. If I am a dysfunctional person and you are a functional person and we decide to become a couple, we will still have a dysfunctional relationship because dysfunction is present. If I am a dysfunctional person and likewise you are also dysfunctional, we are guaranteed to have a dysfunctional relationship if we pursue love and commitment with each other.

You should be 100% as an individual before you become 50% of a couple.

As long as dysfunction is present in any kind of relationship, it will be a dysfunctional one. The only way to be a functional couple is for both parties involved to be functional individuals. If your objective is to be in a

FUNCTIONAL, HAPPY, and MONOGAMOUS relationship with someone, you must first be functional individuals, who find someone who has also done the necessary work on themselves, and has become functional him or herself. If you are aware of your dysfunction(s), then you have already conquered half of the battle. Once you have acknowledged the problem, it can be fixed. The introspective work must now begin, which may not be an easy thing to do, but it is very achievable—if you choose to achieve it. This journey is a must, if you realistically expect to ever take part in a functional relationship.

It's unfortunate, and most probable, to look directly to your left or right and find someone who has some sort of dysfunctional issue they need to tend to. There are so many people who walk around every day, burdened with loads of baggage stemmed from their childhood or from the curve balls life often throws.

An unhealthy you equals an unhealthy relationship. Work on healing the inner you.

As sensible as this philosophy may be, some people will still come up with an "excuse" for not "fixing" their dysfunctional selves before getting into a relationship, but they will try. They will continue wasting time and happiness, hoping that they will be the first who proves that $1 + 1$ can equal 3. Well, it doesn't. They're just not mentally ready to do the hard work it takes to become the best version of themselves. That's how powerful the land of denial can be. No matter how much you may want or believe 1 + 1 should equal to 3, it doesn't. The reality is, it equals 2. The longer it takes for you to address the core of your dysfunctional behaviors, the longer you will be without the type of relationship you desire to be in. You can spend the rest of your life trying to disprove this ideology and continue being a part of the 80 percent of people who are in failing or failed relationships; or you can opt for a challenging experience, which will serve you much better in the long run.

I was in an accident a few years ago, which resulted in me having two herniated discs in my lumbar spine. Because the discs are resting on my sciatic nerve, I have a constant shooting pain down my butt cheek and leg. Now, there is a remedy for this pain, but in order for me to "fix" this problem, I will have to go through more pain. I have to get three to five, 3-inch needles stuck into my spine, without an anesthetic. As you can imagine, this is a very painful procedure, but I do have options. I can continue with the daily sciatic pain or I can go through the 15-minute painful procedure and have all five needles stuck into my body, which will ultimately end my sciatic pain. Again, the variables are interchangeable, but the concept is exactly the same.

Sometimes, in order to end one form of pain, you have to go through something else very uncomfortable, in order to resolve the pain you are currently experiencing. Before one goes to heaven, one must die. You can't have one without the other. There's simply no way around it. Similarly, if you want to have a functional relationship, you must face the original pain you've experienced, which is most likely the cause of your current dysfunctional behaviors. You must get to the source in order to find out what causes you to have a negative impact on your relationships.

There is no way around not fixing yourself, if having a happy, functional, monogamous relationship is your objective. The journey may be uncomfortable, but the discomfort will be temporary and will end the moment you accept your past as part of your reality; then and only then will you begin to heal.

This is the juncture where I believe most people have trouble, and I feel like it's the most important hurdle to get over. We can sometimes be our harshest critics, but when it comes to admitting our wrongs and our faults and actually admitting we need help, that's quite the challenge. Just imagine if everyone could admit to their imperfections and have the discipline to fix whatever it is they need fixed to capture the best version of themselves. Can you imagine how light this world would be? Less anger, less jealousy, less selfishness and much more of the opposite.

Your journey through life will not always be pleasant or easy. Sometimes the road to your destination may be a bit bumpy, but you still need to get to where you need to be. Don't allow that to be a deterrent. You have to find the discipline needed to stay on the bumpy road, even though at times you may be tempted to take a detour. Fight hard to get to that desired destination, which is to find and keep the happiness you want to share with the perfect one for you. No more wasting time by offering anyone the lesser version of your best self, and no more accepting folks who are offering you the lesser versions of their best selves. The longer you are with Mr. or Ms. Wrong, the longer you will be without Mr. or Ms. Right. Do the work necessary to bring you closer to the person you want to spend the rest of your life with, happily.

Because many people find difficulty in regressing to a time of unhappiness and pain, it is usually not done. So the irony is that many who are searching for love are a big part of the reason why it can't be found. I'm harping on this point specifically because it's a step that cannot be skipped, and I believe it will be the most challenging obstacle for most people to embrace. It is common sense, really. If you accept the fact that you have anger, jealousy issues or abusive tendencies, the inability to be faithful—although you would like to be—or any other characteristic that impedes you from maintaining a happy, functional, monogamous relationship must be recognized. Even if you find yourself to be accepting of people who offer the same dysfunctional behaviors, you must conquer the step of finding out why! If this isn't something you're ready to do, the rest of this book will be of no positive service to you. You will only continue giving and receiving the same dysfunction as you have been thus far. If you want to bake a different cake, you must use different ingredients. If you don't, you will be baking the same old cake.

The next chapter will support my belief in the importance of changing whatever damaging behaviors prior to getting into a serious relationship with somem statistics. Overall, the numbers aren't pretty, but they don't have to be this way. The increase to more successful relationships can start with you; so let's make it happen!

Chapter 4

Statistics

For as long as I can remember, I've always been a lover of love. I can't think of anything better or greater than this phenomenal emotion. If I had to choose between having an unlimited amount of funds in the bank, fleets of cars parked in the garages of all of the mansions I own all over the world, or being blessed with meeting the woman of my dreams, who provides most of my wants, and satisfies all of my needs ... finding the true love of my life, who genuinely and functionally loves me, as I do her, I would choose love every time.

Anyone who truly understands how powerful this emotion is or anyone who has experienced it will tell you nothing compares to the blissful feeling of loving someone, who reciprocates the same level of emotion. Soul singer Al Green truly captured the power of love in his lyric when he said, "love will make you come home early or make you stay out all night long." Wars have started over love. People are willing to kill and die to protect someone they love, which makes my next point so ironic. Love is something that is greatly desired and needed by the masses, yet tragically, it's also the most abused commodity that's taken for granted by the same masses. Go figure! Love doesn't cost a penny, but its value is priceless. The potential to be "rich" is inside each and every one of us, yet so many choose to squander this blessing.

Anchored Relationships

Statistics show that nearly 60 percent of couples who get married end up in divorce court. This leaves a remaining balance of 40 percent of couples who are still technically married, but of this 40 percent, half of those couples are what I refer to as "anchored" in their relationships. Which means, they are tethered to a relationship they would otherwise be completely free from. They feel cemented in their situation and feel compelled to remain in this unwanted, unhappy relationship for a plethora of reasons.

The anchor could be history: "We've been together for 15 years! I'm not going anywhere and neither is he/she." Or, "We have kids together, who are still in school, and a mortgage, so it's much cheaper for me to keep her!" Tragically, this means only 10 to 20 percent out of 100 couples are actually happy in their relationship. This is a terribly unfortunate statistic, and if you doubt the accuracy of these numbers, please take a moment and really think about how many couples you personally know of who are truly happy in their relationship and compare them to the number of couples you know of who aren't happy with their significant other. You will find the overwhelming majority will go to the unhappy couples.

This tells us that at least 80 percent of couples, those who have divorced, plus those who are anchored or stuck in their relationship, are not experiencing love the way it is meant to be given and received. These statistics, plus your personal experiences, along with what you've witnessed with other couples, are the strongest indicators of an imminent need for a change in the way we pursue and endure relationships. We have been doing something wrong, and it would be insane to continue the same practices if a different result is desired.

If you had a car that broke down 80 percent of the time you drove it, you would either have it "fixed" or get another car. Even if you decided to continue driving it, you would naturally feel terribly insecure behind the wheel because of the car's unpredictability and unreliability. You may not be in a financial position to purchase a reliable car at the time you deem it to be unsafe, so perhaps being without a car for the moment will be a healthier, safer, less stressful option for you versus continuing to drive a car that's dangerously unreliable and is guaranteed to completely fail at some point. Why wouldn't this same logic be applied to dysfunctional relationships? I'll illustrate the comparison by using the same scenario, but I will interchange the two variables by substituting the broken car and replacing it with a broken relationship, and you will see how the concept remains exactly the same.

If you had a (car) relationship that broke down 80 percent of the time, you would either fix it or simply get into a better (car) relationship. Even if you decided to (drive it) endure it, you would naturally feel terribly insecure the entire time you're inside of that (car) relationship. Perhaps, at this time, you are unable to (purchase a replacement car) get into another relationship, and at the moment, being (without a car) single will be a healthier, safer, less stressful option for you, versus continuing to (drive a car) endure a relationship that's full of unreliability and is guaranteed to completely fail at some point. Sometimes a car gets so beat up, mistreated and misused, it's rundown and beyond repair. The same with some relationships.

Most people wouldn't drive a car that breaks down 80 percent of the time, for fear of it causing an accident or because of the potential dangers it may bring to them or to someone else. Why don't we use the same precaution when it comes to our hearts? Why do you tend to stay in broken relationships, which will inevitably hurt you or someone else? If you customarily bake apple pies, and now you want to start making cherry pies, you absolutely have to change the fruit. Without the change, you're guaranteed to end up with the same apple pie you've always baked. We've all made the mistake of doing the same thing and hoping for or expecting a different result.

This mistake is way too common, and it's one we should really focus on changing.

We have heard all of our lives that relationships are difficult and require a lot of work. I don't subscribe to this ideology at all. Actually, I totally reject this notion, which I believe is partially responsible for people entertaining foiled relationships for longer periods of time than they should. This belief sets you up for failure, as it doesn't allow you to adhere to the red flags and dysfunction that are oftentimes demonstrated early on in the relationship. In a sense, it encourages you to accept or work through these red flags because there is that voice inside that reassures you that no relationship is perfect, so keep fighting and enduring, no matter what.

Obviously, this is an option, but when it is evident that the level of dysfunction is profound and there are many levels of discord in the relationship, fighting to make it work will not bring you toward "destination happiness" anytime soon, if ever. If you are unhappy and, 15 or 20 years from now, you find that you are a happy couple, if you reflect back, you will see that you have both either changed the dysfunctional behavior or have simply acquiesced to it. Only bad/wrong relationships require a lot of work, positive/good ones don't. Good relationships are healthy and fruitful, which should flow organically. They are fluid and seamless and should be productive, not counterproductive. When you choose to become involved with someone and the best parts of you are being stripped away, while the worst parts seem to flourish, you are definitely with the wrong person. Your significant other should not be the one who brings out the darkest parts of you. They should be the one who shines light on to the darkness, which eradicates it, just as light does to the dark. We absolutely need to reevaluate how we pursue good love and how we endure bad "love." Most importantly, we need to be able to differentiate between the two.

Once you have become the best possible version of yourself, you will understand your worth, and you won't settle for anything less than what you know you deserve. The beauty about being this self-aware is twofold. Not only will you realize when you are selling yourself short by being with someone who doesn't fulfill you, but you will also recognize when you are not giving or won't be able to give yourself to someone, for whatever reason. Even though that person may genuinely want a relationship with you, you will still be able to walk away without feeling any obligation or guilt.

Many of us have been there before, where we have stayed in relationships with someone, simply because they've expressed a sincere interest in making us happy, even though we don't reciprocate the same level of natural interest. Or, initially there was an interest, but then for whatever reason, the excitement fizzled, and we didn't feel as though there was a "good enough reason" to sever the romantic ties with this person.

I remember being in a relationship with someone many years ago, which initially was fantastic. She was beautiful, we had gotten along great, and I even remember thinking to myself, *If this vibe remains the same, I think she just might be the one!* Welp, the vibe changed, and I no longer had the desire to continue dating her as I had the months before. My dilemma was that I didn't feel like I had a valid "reason" to break up with her, so I began searching for one. I eventually found what I was looking for and broke up with her, even though in truth, my "reason" was quite silly. I felt because she was a sweet girl and I didn't want to hurt her feelings, I needed to have what I considered to be a "valid" reason to end the relationship. I am now aware that simply wanting to break up because of not being content is all the reasoning I need to get out of a relationship I am not happy in.

When it's Time to Move On

Regardless of how long you have been together, once you KNOW the person you are with no longer provides what you need in order to be happy, then it is time to move on. I have been told many times, that it's not always that easy, and I absolutely agree. For example, I have a friend who has been with her husband for 15 years and married for 11. They have two small children, a beautiful house with the proverbial picket fence and great careers. But, she is no longer happy with her husband, and she desperately wants to be. She has told me that she is no longer in love with him, but they are good friends and loves him as a person. I am sure you can imagine how anchored she feels to this relationship. Breaking up the family will put a great deal of guilt on her heart, so for the sake of her kids, the benefit of having two incomes and not wanting to feel like a "failure," she feels compelled to stay in her marriage.

The Path to Happiness

As previously stated, there are more couples than not who are in similar difficult situations. I have shared with her what I believe her options are, and none of them are easy decisions to make. They can go to couple's therapy and see if that will benefit their marriage, but she doesn't believe therapy is the answer, as she feels as though she has genuinely fallen out of love with him. They can also divorce, hopefully amicably, and co-parent as best as they possibly can from separate households. Or they can divorce and parent from the same household, as in having an open relationship. After speaking with her in-depth, the only option she feels that would make her the happiest relationship-wise would be a divorce. I've included her story to illustrate how difficult the path to happiness can be, but you must fight to stay on the bumpy road in order to arrive to "destination happiness."

Just because happiness is possible, it doesn't mean that getting there will be easy. There may be broken hearts involved—and not necessarily limited to the couples involved. Children, in-laws and close family and friends are sometimes deeply impacted by breakups. But, at the end of the day, how THEY feel about you staying in your unhappy marriage bares no significance. Not if your objective is for you and your spouse to be happy, and you see no path to that reality as a couple—do what you have to do that best ensures your path to being happy. Anyone who is negatively affected by your decision has to find a way to get over their disappointment.

Chapter 5

Being Alone is Better than Having Someone & Being Lonely

Loneliness and solitude can be very scary notions for people who aren't truly happy within themselves, and also for those who have not yet mastered the concept of acceptance. Once you're able to truly experience happiness from the inside out, and can absolutely enjoy your own company, you will not settle for a spouse who doesn't provide you with the same level of tranquility that you provide for yourself. Allowing someone to enter your life to disrupt the peace you've established will no longer be an option, and you will be perfectly fine with rejecting anyone you know isn't right for you. This is the personal growth you should be seeking versus revisiting history and allowing negative energy to be a part of your life, partly for the sake of not being alone. You would have learned a life-changing lesson, which is, being a happy person starts within you; and being single is always a much better option than being a miserable person with a spouse right next to you.

One of the major reasons why people endure dysfunctional relationships is because of a real fear of being alone. "I don't want to grow old alone!" How many times have you heard that quote recited? How many times have you said it yourself? It's perfectly normal to conjure up scenarios of how you're going to meet the love of your life or to romanticize about whom will be the lucky person you're going to spend the rest of your life with. But, allowing these thoughts to consume you, or to negatively alter your mood or state of being for not having it is certainly unhealthy and absolutely futile. It's a battle you should choose not to engage in, as it's a fight you have zero control over.

If we had the power or control to be with whomever we wanted, whenever we wanted, we would all be enjoying happy, functional, monogamous relationships at our will. The truth is, we have no idea when or even if we are going to find our soul mates in this incarnation, so it would behoove us to live this blessed lifetime as happily and as productively as possible. And if we don't know how to do so, we should make it a priority to learn how to. This is critical for the sake of our sanity, as well as our physical health.

Too many people stress themselves about not being in a happy, functional, monogamous relationship, while allowing depression and sadness to find a place in their lives because of it. This is very unfortunate, because the energy expended worrying about something they have no control over can be directed in other areas of their lives, which would ultimately help them be better prepared for when they do encounter the love they so desire. Worrying about when you're going to find true love is equally pointless as worrying about when or how we are going to die. Unless it's self-inflicted, the when and how of our deaths are beyond our control, and this is why we go about living our lives until that fateful day arises. Once we can accept the fact that we are not in control of finding the love we seek, just as we aren't in control of our inevitable deaths, is when we will be less inclined to worry about the when and how of meeting that love. We will begin to live life without worry, without pain and without fear! Acceptance of this fact will go a long way, in many ways.

Loneliness is an actual thing, as there are people in this world who, for whatever reason, have no one in their lives to count on to fill that void. There's no doubt that we certainly thrive off of the energy from other people and when it's not received for a long period of time, it can drive a sane man crazy. Solitude and isolation is so intense that they are often used as forms of torture. Solitary confinement is commonly practiced in prisons to discipline inmates, and of course, very long periods of separation from other people for prisoners of war.

Have you seen the movie *Cast Away* starring Tom Hanks? After being the sole survivor of an airplane crash, he found himself completely alone on an island for several years, until he came across an old, beat-up volleyball, which he cleverly named Wilson. He drew facial features on Wilson and suddenly he had a friend to keep him company. Wilson didn't say very much, but he happened to be a great listener, and if he had real ears, they would have been talked off. Although Wilson wasn't an actual person, the ball now occupied the space once held by loneliness. It was better than having nothing or no one at all. We aren't too different than the character in this movie. Rather than being alone or feeling lonely, we entertain people who have no business being in our lives. We allow them to drain the best parts of us, instead of bettering the worst parts of us.

Unfortunately, too many of us feel that being with the wrong one is better than being with no one at all.

Denial is usually prevalent in relationships we know are unhealthy for us, but that's the tool we use to keep pushing through the cement wall. We spend more time trying to convince ourselves that things will improve and that we have the stamina to continue the long arduous fight we've been told we will need in order to keep our relationships going. We do this even when we know and feel in our hearts and souls that the people we allow to break us down and steal our joy really aren't the right ones for us. Unfortunately, too many of us feel that being with the wrong one is better than being with no one at all.

Anyone who feels this way must really be honest with themselves and evaluate their self-esteem and self-worth.

This belief can only exist in those who haven't become one with themselves and are completely oblivious to their unrealized worth. When you are aware of your self-worth, you lead with it in every aspect of your life. Not only with your romantic relationships, but your relationships with friends, family and even co-workers. Doing what's best for your mind, body and soul will be your priority, and it will be non-negotiable.

Just imagine for a second having a 500 credit score. Having this low credit score has negatively impacted your life and has made progress for you seem like an impossibility. This score has prevented you from being able to purchase a home, because the mortgage lenders consider you to be too high risk. Financing a car is possible, but the interest rate would be so high, it would make the car unaffordable. You have even found difficulty in qualifying for another job to help with your finances. Everywhere you turn you bump into the proverbial brick wall and you have had enough. You're finally realizing that this low credit score is your PERSONAL GROWTH STUNTER and you are now committed to getting out of your own way so you can better your life.

You have finally ACKNOWLEDGED that your score needs improvement, and you have ACCEPTED it as your reality. You are now ready to MOVE ON to bigger and better things and have committed to making the necessary strides to significantly improve your score. You decided to seek out a PROFESSIONAL to help FIX your score, which will in turn help you achieve a happier life. For the next year and a half, you worked diligently, following the experts advice to the letter, which ultimately rewards you with a 780 credit score! You will protect and cherish the value of that score and do everything in your power to maintain or improve it.

Remembering where your credit score was just 1.5 years prior and the tremendous work you put in to get to that respectable score, if someone asked you to co-sign a car for them, would you do it? What would you say to them when they ask?? A resounding HELL NO!! Absolutely not, right?! Because you know the difficulties you had with such a low score and what you had gone through in order to bring yourself UP to this level, and that you are aware of it's WORTH, you will not allow anyone to bring you back down.

One you have gone through the process of bringing yourself UP from a place of pain, dysfunction, dissatisfaction and unhappiness, you will not allow anyone else to bring you down. Once you are aware of your self-worth and you begin to self-love and your esteem level is at an all-time high, you will protect it and not ALLOW anyone to interrupt your new found being. This is where you should always be; either maintaining it or improving it.

Loving yourself should be your main priority if you ever expect someone else to love you properly.

The reality is, many people who are in taxing, dysfunctional relationships, usually feel alone or lonely, even though they have a spouse right next to them on a daily basis. They aren't receiving or haven't been giving the love, attention, conversation or even the beautiful silence happy couples exchange with each other. Having a physical body in your immediate space will not necessarily make you feel the euphoric fulfillment and completion people who are in great, loving relationships feel.

Whenever you are in a problematic relationship, you are doing yourself and anyone involved with it a disservice. Again, we are taught that relationships are difficult and require a lot of work, but I contend that only bad/wrong relationships are difficult and require a lot of work, not good/right ones. If you were to get into your car and turn the key in the ignition and the engine doesn't turn over, you would say that the car doesn't work. The car won't move or take you where you need to be, as long as it is not working. If you were to keep trying over and over again and the starter never sparks, you have a car that doesn't work. It's useless to you. The more time you spend trying to get this useless, broken-down car to turn over is the more time you're spending away from reaching your destination, correct? The same concept applies to relationships. I am not suggesting to run away at the first sign of trouble, but I am saying that happiness is an option and if the person you are with does not make you happy there are other choices.

I have found that there are more couples who spend more time trying to make their relationships work than their relationships actually working. The more time you spend with Mr./Ms. Wrong is the more time you'll spend away from Mr./Ms. Right. It's like trying to fit a square peg into a round hole. You can relentlessly bang the peg with great determination to make it fit into the hole, and ultimately some parts of the peg will get in, but there will be a significant amount of damage done to the peg from all the banging and determination. These dents, splinters, and broken pieces of the peg represent the fights, infidelities and insecurities found in relationships that couples spend so much time trying to fix.

If you have noticed from your personal experiences and those of your family members and friends, the vast majority of couples who have spent most of their relationships trying to fix or make it work ultimately end up separating or they give up and give in to the unhappiness. The only time a broken relationship can be fixed is if the person or persons with the dysfunctional traits work on their "issues" individually. If not, their dysfunctional actions will continually resurface, not remedying, but exacerbating the problems in the relationship.

I have been preaching this sermon to my friends for many years, and I'm usually met with resistance. My favorite and most common one is, "I'm going to pray on it!" Or, they will come back with, "Well, if we really love each other, we can make it work," or "If he/she really loves me, they will change." These are more of the falsehoods we have been made to believe as truths, and to our detriment most of us believe them. My retort to that is, "What's love got to do with it?"

There are people in divorce court every day who are still IN love with each other, but they know within their heart of hearts that they can no longer be together, if being happy is part of their agenda. They can no longer do it, not even for the "sake" of their children or the peripherals in their lives, whose desire for them to remain together far surpasses their own. Maybe someone betrayed the other's trust, or perhaps they've just grown in different directions. In either of these particular instances, one would have to give up a part of themselves in order to be with the other person. One may have to be in a relationship with someone they no longer trust, and the other would have to sacrifice the path of their own life in order to commit to the direction their partner has gravitated toward. Staying together in either example are disasters waiting to happen, because you will inevitably be losing a part of yourself in the process of "trying to make it work."

Before we can truly love anyone else, we must first be able to truly love ourselves. I can't stress this point enough. There is just no way around this philosophy, although many try to defy it. If you have ever flown on an airplane, you should be aware that the flight attendant always instructs that in the case of an emergency, the first thing for you to do is to place your oxygen mask over your face before you help anyone else with theirs, including your own children. Again, you are no good to anyone if you are no good to yourself. Loving yourself is a prerequisite to loving anyone else.

I know the first instinct for many of you reading this is to disagree with many of the ideologies I am sharing that may bring you some discomfort or anxiety, but before you do, I want you to think about what we have covered thus far.

1) Approximately 60 percent of couples who get married end up in divorce. Half of the remaining 40 percent are unhappy in their relationship, which means the majority of us are doing something wrong when it comes to pursuing and enduring relationships.

2) Based on these statistics, we know that we have been taught to love and endure love incorrectly, and if we want to join those who are truly happy in their relationships, things must be done differently.

3) In order for us to love anyone happily, functionally and monogamously, we must first love ourselves completely.

So, please, before you revert back to your old way of thinking of how we should be loving each other, please remember its flaws and proven, unsuccessful outcomes. Remain focused to a different, more efficient way of loving each other and how to pursue a happy, functional, monogamous relationship. Please keep your mind open to change.

Chapter 6

Hope Keeps Us Alive

Hope is probably my third most favorite English word, preceded by love and acceptance, respectively. Hope is defined as a feeling of expectation and desire for a certain thing to happen. Hope is also synonymous with wish, but I do believe there is a subtle difference between the two. For instance, you can "wish someone would" or wish upon a star or wish for your lottery numbers to hit, but if for whatever reason none of the things you are wishing for come to fruition, you won't be too lost or devastated by it. Wishing is more of a fantasy you would like to see come to pass versus hope being much more profound.

The power of hope can easily be seen as our one little miracle, tucked away deep inside of each and every one of us. It's an omnipresent reserve we tap into when we want an expectation or desire of ours to be manifested into our reality. "Keep hope alive," is commonly suggested, because for so many of us, that's exactly what it does. It energizes and flashes us with endless positive possibilities, attainable to the one who is full of hope. In times of despair or when you feel like you're at the end of your rope, hope has a way of reassuring you that you are still in the fight. If you can someway, somehow focus with all of your fervor and with all of your might, whatever it is you are hopeful for, you can "miraculously" manifest it into existence.

Personally, I don't necessarily believe the miracle is found in the actual manifestation of your desire, but rather in the getting through of another day, which may have otherwise seemed impossible to do without hope playing its part. Hope is absolutely vital to most of our existence, as it provides us with the strength and light to make it through the darkest of places. There have been many who have lost or have given up on their ability to hope, which equated to them forgoing their will to live. Keeping hope alive can quite literally keep us alive to fight another day. With hope, you believe you can see the light at the end of the tunnel, and it can provide the necessary strength to keep reaching for it. What kind of life is livable if you are hopeless?

The manifestation of hope is akin to a tag-teamed, coordinated effort between your mind, body, spirit and God. You can hope to lose 20 pounds by the summer, but if you don't implement a diet and/or exercise program to ensure your success, you're really just "wishing" to lose 20 pounds by the summer. Hope requires mental, physical or spiritual action, or all of the above, depending on your desire. The differences between being hopeful or being wishful are very subtle, yet significantly profound.

Anything you want to accomplish, or any goal or standard you have set for yourself, can certainly be obtained, if you have the mental fortitude, commitment and desire, which should provide you with the strength needed to remain focused and to do the things required in order to be successful at achieving your goal. You have total control over your input to accomplishing the goals you set for yourself and zero control over anyone else's desire. Being hopeful for someone else's success can be tricky, because you must relinquish all of the control over to him or her.

Hope must be coupled with action, and you cannot make anyone do anything they cannot, or will not do. We all know we can bring a horse to water, but we can't make him take a sip. Expecting someone to have your level of desire can be detrimental to accomplishing whatever it is you are hopeful to achieve. Accomplishing your dreams is possible, because you are in total control of doing the work that is required of you. You can choose to do the work or not. It's a completely different ball game when it comes to any dream or aspiration you may have, which involves someone else's success. This includes, but is not limited to, a partner you hope to share with a happy, functional, monogamous relationship.

If you are in a relationship that is suffering and you desperately want to save it, you can put forth all of the energy you have to breathe life back into it, but if your partner doesn't have the same level of commitment or greater, you are simply wasting your very precious time. The depths of love you have for someone is simply not enough to sustain a failing relationship, if they do not provide you with what you NEED in order to be happy.

"Love conquers all" is another misguided mantra too many people have subscribed to, and have proven this motto to be false, over and over again. Love can be a motivator to change things for the better, but it is not the absolute remedy. If the love and desire you have motivates you to do all the necessary things to fix what is broken, but your spouse isn't meeting you halfway, the outcome will most likely be a bleak one. Regardless of your determination and will, if your spouse is not pulling their weight, there will be no progression. Together you are a team, divided – you are individuals. You must work together, if you want to achieve the same goals, which are happiness, functionality and monogamy.

Playing as a Team

Imagine that you and your spouse are teammates playing a two-against-two basketball game. A missed shot is made and you both jump to grab the rebound. You are both tugging and FIGHTING to win possession of the ball, which is counterproductive to you winning the game as a team. Winning the game is what's important, and that can only be accomplished if you play as a team and not as individuals. You must communicate effectively with each play you make. Sometimes you have to pass your spouse the ball and other times you will receive a pass from your spouse, in order for a shot to be made. When the shot is made, you both score as a team, not as individuals. If both players on the team are not willing to play as a coordinated, selfless teammate, they will have a dysfunctional game. If you have a spouse who doesn't want to be or is incapable of being a team player, you have to determine if it is best for you to start playing 1-on-1 games, or if you should look for another partner, who is willing to play as a team. Your choice to continue playing or not is your power, so don't foolishly waste it. Again, you can bring a horse to water, but you cannot make him drink. Trying to change this fact is futile, so please don't waste your time attempting to do so.

I have spoken with plenty of people who are unhappy in their relationship, and some of them have decided to just sit back and leave it all in the hands of God to "heal" it. Or, they have convinced themselves that once their significant other sees the effort they are putting in to make the relationship work, they will follow suit. That's another false narrative we've blindly followed, although it has all proven to be wildly inaccurate. Both parties must have the desire or hope to stay together, and if that is not the case, the relationship should be deemed hopeless.

Being hopeful for a broken relationship to be fixed is absolutely a realistic possibility, if both parties want the relationship to be rekindled and are willing to do the work required to fix it. This is being realistic. On the other hand, pursuing a relationship where the glaring red flags are too obvious to ignore, yet you try to anyway, is not being hopeful, it's simply pursuing a fantasy. Pursuing an emotional fantasy usually does not end well if you plan on living it out in the realm of reality. It does not match.

One evening I had gone to a little gathering a friend of mine was hosting at his home, and I decided to bring a platonic friend with me, who I will call Lisa, for company. Once we arrived, I rang the doorbell and when my friend, the host, opened the door, I couldn't help but notice the stars, hearts and bright beams of light emanating from the eyes of my accompanying friend as she struggled to subdue her attraction to him. When we entered his home, I introduced them to each other, and through her very conspicuous gaze at him, I could literally feel her wondering what they were going to name their first-born child. Immediately after he took our coats and told us that his casa was our casa, Lisa turned to me and said, "I've finally met my future husband!" I giggled and replied, "Absolutely not!" I told her that he is a fun guy, but he is most definitely not "relationship material." I explained to her that for the 15 years I had known him, he had never been a one woman's man and was actually quite proud of it. He had mentioned on many occasions that monogamy was not something he was interested in practicing, which is perfectly fine, as long as everyone involved is aware of his preference and agrees with it.

Unfortunately, he was notorious for not being very forthcoming or truthful about his relationship practices and beliefs. He was often misleading and did and said whatever he had to in order to get whatever it is he wanted. She insisted that perhaps he felt and acted that way because he hadn't met the right woman and was completely convinced that she was the woman who would change his practices, mindset and lifestyle. I told her I was very aware of many of his extracurricular activities, and how he treats women doesn't align with what she had expressed she needs from a man. Before the end of the night was over, the two of them had exchanged numbers and had their first date already planned.

One afternoon my phone rang. I answered it, and on the other end of the line was Lisa sobbing and crying hysterically. After I was able to calm her down, she told me she found out that he was "cheating" on her with two other women. She went on to tell me how he took advantage of her heart and how devastated she is by his betrayal. She was given an ear full of facts and a list of examples as to why it was in her best interest to not pursue a romantic relationship with this guy. Quite honestly, I was perplexed by her shock and dismay, regarding his transgressions. I couldn't understand how she could feel the way she felt, when she KNEW exactly what it was that he had to offer, because I was crystal clear when I told her.

I'm sure she felt it wasn't the best time for me to ask her if she remembered me strongly suggesting for her to stay away from him, but I did anyway. The point of the matter is that she isn't alone. Far too many people choose a person they want to be the right one for them, even though all signs point to them not being a good match. She was guilty of doing what she wanted to do, versus doing what she should have done, which was to not date him.

Many people, including Lisa have told me that they feel like they have to go through things in order for them to learn from the experience, which simply isn't true. What they are really saying is they just want to do what they want to do and let the cards fall where they may. If I had told Lisa that she shouldn't play in the street with oncoming, speeding cars, I'm quite positive she wouldn't do it. Why wouldn't she need to have that experience in order to learn that lesson?

The signs are always there. When someone first shows you who they are, believe them. The issue is that many overlook the red flags or think they can change a person. Never think for once you can change a person.

People pick and choose what they want to experience and how they will experience it. Lisa chose to date someone she knew went completely against the grain of what she knew she could handle in a relationship. Realistically, Lisa's heartache was absolutely her fault.

She was given all of the information she needed about him to make an informed decision, which she did. I'm sure this may seem harsh to some, but we must be accountable for our actions and when to recognize and place blame where it needs to be placed. We need to learn when to use our pointer finger or our thumb for blame placement, and to take full responsibility when need be.

Sometimes when we get hurt, we are quick to say how someone else has hurt us, when oftentimes our choices, like Lisa's, is what caused our pain, not the other person. If Lisa had accompanied me to a friend's house who had their dog in its crate, and I told her not to pet the dog under any circumstance because it will bite anyone it's not familiar with, and she ignores my warning and gets bitten after sticking her hand in the crate, is it the dog's fault for doing what dogs do? Or is it her fault for ignoring the warning? I believe it's the latter. She wouldn't have gotten hurt by my friend if she had chosen not to date him because of the information she had learned about him. Just as, she wouldn't have gotten bitten if she hadn't stuck her hand it the crate of a dog who was known to bite strangers. Lisa decided to live in a fantasy world, until reality set in. She could have learned that lesson without having to go through that hurtful experience, but it was her choice to do so.

Many of us have entertained dating people we know aren't good for us. Sometimes they may even be a good catch, but for someone else. If you start to date someone new, and you find yourself saying how perfect they would be if only they would change this or had more of that or was less of the other, what you are essentially saying is, you want to date a different person. Entering into a relationship like this is guaranteed to breed dissatisfaction into your life. Anyone who ignores the dangers of doing this and chooses to live on this fantasy island will certainly have disappointment visit them sooner than later. Remember, if your objective is to have a happy, functional, monogamous relationship, there are just certain things you can't do and certain things you need to do.

Waiting Can Be Rewarding

Patience truly is a virtue, and I can assure you that waiting patiently for the right person for you beats living with all of the problems that are inherently a part of a dysfunctional relationship. Do not live in a world of fantasy. Progress yourself in this realm of reality! If it doesn't fit, it doesn't fit. If it's not right, it's not right. Pretending that it is does not make it so. All you're doing is making a choice to hurt yourself, which is an option you don't have to take. What I hope you are receiving from this chapter is, it is one thing to have hope of one day meeting the person who captures all of the qualities you need in order for you to be happy in a relationship. It is another thing to believe you can change the personality and character traits of anyone and morph them into the person you NEED for them to be, in order for YOU to be happy. Any attempt to change who a person is, in order for them to fit your standard of a potential mate is a recipe for a disaster and further demonstrates that person isn't the right one for you, or else you wouldn't be trying to change them.

Chapter 7

Respect & Ego Don't Mix

I would absolutely be remiss, if while discussing the failure of relationships, I didn't speak specifically about respect. Respect, or the lack thereof, is certainly one of the main reasons why relationships aren't as harmonious as they should be. I see and speak to lots of people who are in relationships, and claim to be in love with the ones they are with, but something I fail to see in many cases is respect. How can you be in love with someone and not have respect as the foundation for you to build on?

I believe when two people get together, fall in love and decide to commit to each other, there is a certain way they should agree to act and speak to each other. There should be an understanding that they are now a unit, and there are certain things they must be cognizant of, if they want to maintain a high level of integrity in the relationship. Everything they say and do pertaining to each other should always be prefaced with respect. When the respect for each other diminishes, so will the integrity. Then what?

When a man considers his woman to be his Queen, and when a woman considers her man to be her King, the way they act toward each other should reflect that sentiment. Expecting to be treated like a King or a Queen when you have peasant-like behaviors is unrealistic. When your spouse treats you like you are on a pedestal, and you are reciprocating that same treatment, you have a much greater chance of having a special bond with your spouse, than if you didn't consistently demonstrate the level of respect you will need in order to accomplish this kind of treatment.

Generational Belief Systems

I have said this to couples before and I have been told, more than once I might add, that I am living in a fantasy world. Really? Spouses putting each other on a pedestal is unrealistic? Nope, it's not. We just haven't been taught that's how it should be. What we have been taught is, "we hurt the ones closest to us" or "relationships are hard." This is the generational B.S. we have been fed and we have been eating it all up. I believe when you are in a functional space, you protect and love the ones you love. I further believe that wrong relationships are hard. When it's right they aren't. We must rid ourselves of generational B.S.

Wouldn't it be great if the person you truly loved put you on a pedestal? Just imagine the quality of the relationship you would have if you did the same. When I mention treating your spouse like a King or Queen, I don't mean that you genuflect whenever they pass by, or to fan them with peacock feathers, while feeding them fruit as they relax. I simply mean that your actions towards them makes them feel as if you actually do these things.

Do you know what the difference between having an argument and a disagreement is? Simply, your tone of voice. In both cases you are having an opposing opinion or perspective, but the way it is handled preserves the integrity of the relationship, and if being happy, functional and monogamous is your objective, maintaining the integrity of your relationship is imperative.

When the respect you have for your spouse stays on a high pedestal and it is reciprocated, ANYTHING that falls under the umbrella of lies, deceit or mistrust will never be a part of your relationship. Disrespectful tones and words chip away at the integrity of your relationship. The more fights and arguments you have versus discussions and disagreements, the less you will respect your partner, which will inevitably manifest into disrespectful actions.

Would you ever tell your grandmother or your clergyman to shut up, while using descriptive expletives? I'm assuming that you wouldn't. You wouldn't do that because of the RESPECT that you have for them, right? Why would you then do that to your "King or Queen?" The more you chip away at the integrity of your relationship, the more difficult it is to mend back those precious pieces. Late apologies and gifts won't do it.

As I stated earlier, if you expect to be treated like a King or a Queen, you have to be worthy of that kind of treatment. This is what I find to be so amazing about this philosophy. Respect is a gauge that couples should use to keep themselves accountable for their words and actions. It creates checks and balances and if you follow them, your relationship should be just fine. In other words, if you are always mindful of what you say and do, whether your spouse is right next to you or not, that helps you stay within the confines of having a respectful relationship. Anyone who doesn't feel there should be confines or limitations to their relationships, simply wants to do their own thing, which would be perfectly fine, if you have a spouse who feels the exact same way. But, for the purpose of speaking on behalf of people who expect to be monogamous, confines and boundaries are essential to maintaining a respectful union.

Remember, when you have decided to engage in a committed relationship, you should no longer expect to have the same mind-set or the ability to do the same things you did when you were single. I firmly believe that whatever actions you should engage in, you should act as if your spouse is right next to you. If they would have a problem with you doing or saying whatever it is you want to do or say, then that is the gauge or the deciding factor that you should adhere to. Practicing this could quite literally save your relationship.

For some, I know it's hard to imagine not ever "blowing up" on your spouse, if they have done something that has absolutely upset you. If you have to blow up when you're upset, I think that's something you need to look into internally, as an individual. If you aren't at the point in your life to where you are able to control your anger, you will most certainly be disrespectful to the one that you love.

Any couple that wants to stay together for as long as their lifetime permits, should always keep respect at the forefront of their minds. Whatever actions they perform, whatever words they may say should be accompanied with respect.

Learning to Respect Yourself

Before you can have this high level of respect for your spouse, you must first have it for yourself. Not enough can be said about having a high regard for yourself. When you are self-aware and truly care about the way you portray yourself to others, or how you are seen by others, your actions will follow accordingly. Being in a place where you can genuinely say that you love your authentic self and you respect who you are, regardless of where you have been or what you have been through, is truly an amazing feeling. When you clearly recognize that you are worthy of your own love, regardless of what you have done in your past, or what has been done to you, you have accomplished something that many people fail to achieve. I do not believe that love can be present without respect.

Getting to this place of self-love and self-respect may require bravery and fortitude on your part. You may have to revisit unpleasant memories in order to get to the root of your self-hate, anger or why the lack of respect for yourself or others exists. But, I can assure you, that respecting your spouse in tone and in action, genuinely, and consistently, whether or not they are in your presence will ONLY be possible, when you have that same high level of respect for yourself. There is no way around it. Similarly, as discussed in previous chapters, you cannot truly love anyone else, until you truly love yourself. Fighting this law is simply a futile battle and a huge waste of time.

EGO - The Three Lettered Demon

EGO - The three lettered demon! This is exactly how I define the ego. Anywhere you find dysfunction, chaos, anger, jealousy, vindictiveness, hate, or just down-right ugly behavior, most times you will find the ego nearby. The ego is not your friend, and should not be treated as such. It is absolutely the enemy and unfortunately, it is too accessible and so close to you.

I speak about "the ego" as if it is its own entity, because it is. It is conniving and manipulative, and it camouflages itself so perfectly, that people actually believe that it is actually THEM. The genius of the ego is that it attaches itself too closely to you that you aren't aware of its existence, and you continue through life, completely unaware of it being there. If you are unaware of its presence, how can you eradicate it? You can't. This is why being able to identify your ego will change how you act and react to situations, as well as how you think.

Being able to identify the ego when it shows its demonic face is key to self-progress. Have you ever noticed that people can be dead wrong about something, but they will defend it to the hilt? There are also those, who can actually admit to being wrong about something, but literally cannot or will not apologize for their wrong doing. Just as living in denial can stunt your growth, so can the ego.

When you are searching for validation from someone, whether it's from a boss, teacher, love interest or from any other person, that's usually your ego wanting to be stroked. When you are adamant about someone seeing and agreeing with your point or perspective, but you can't seem to do the same for them that would be your ego, cheering you on in the background, like a proud parent at a ball game. When you are self-absorbed and your wants and needs always have to be satisfied before you can potentially consider anyone else's, that's your ego showing its ugly head. As you can imagine, anyone who displays the above characteristics will not be able to have a functional, happy, monogamous relationship. Ego is selfish, and it is not kind. It is angry, inconsiderate, self-centered, self-absorbed, possessive and very protective of "its stuff." If you agree with my depiction of the ego, you will also agree that there is no way that someone partnered with an egoist could ever feel equal, special or be put on a pedestal. Likewise, if both people involved were egoists, there definitely couldn't be a relationship that's inclusive, considerate, selfless or RESPECTFUL.

You cannot have love without the presence of respect and you cannot have respect with the presence of ego.

Again, you cannot have love without the presence of respect and you cannot have respect with the presence of ego. I am hoping that you can see how this works. The longer you take to recognize the presence of your ego, the longer it will take for you to become a person, who is consistently respectful to themselves, as well as to others. Therefore, the longer it takes for you to become respectful to yourself and to others, the longer it will be before you are in a happy, functional, respectful, high pedestaled, loving, monogamous relationship.

Everything I have written above, I absolutely believe. It makes perfect sense to me, just as 1+1=2. If you want to have the type of relationship I have been describing in this book, I don't see how it is obtainable without self-love, respect, guidelines, and the suppression of the ego. The combination of all of these things can potentially provide you with the love you've always wanted. Being in this space can absolutely help secure such a relationship, once you have been fortunate enough to find the perfect person for you.

If you are currently in a relationship and would like to continue being with that person, but you do not currently have the type of relationship we have been discussing, then follow all of the steps I have laid out throughout the book. It is absolutely accomplishable, if you both desire to accomplish it. Good luck.

Chapter 8

Wants vs. Needs

Wants versus needs. What an interesting and often conflated dynamic. As I've stated in previous chapters, the vast majority of us are products of dysfunctional homes, and unless these dysfunctional behaviors we have learned are remedied, we will continue to engage in and further teach these traits to others. The only way to stop them dead in their tracks is to recognize and acknowledge these dysfunctional behaviors and do something proactive to eradicate them.

Spending time with a good therapist is the route many people take to help them become the best version of themselves, but not everyone needs to seek help from a professional in order to "fix" themselves. I am in favor of whichever method produces the most positive results. On this journey of becoming the best possible you and tapping into the core of your essence, you will discover many things about yourself, which will be crucial to the success of you entering and sustaining a happy, functional, monogamous relationship.

One of the many things you will discover is how to differentiate between which characteristics you would like or want for your spouse to possess versus what characteristics you need for your spouse to possess. These characteristics are oftentimes confused, as that line can easily be blurred, but it is essential to know the differences between the two. This is where "knowing yourself" comes into play and will be the guide, which will help navigate you away from dead-end relationships. Once you know who you are, you will have learned what your deal breakers are, and you will know when to run for the hills once you meet someone who possesses them.

This will be the new you, breaking the cycle of you trying to fit a square peg into a round hole. You will recognize that the shapes are different, they don't fit together, and you will move on without wasting your precious time. Self-awareness comes with strength and when you are strong, you will allow a deal breaker to be exactly what it is. You will no longer tolerate things that you shouldn't. How many times must your significant other break your deal breakers before they actually become deal breakers? Your answer will be an emphatic once!

Most of us, at some point, have created the proverbial "wish list," which details the characteristics we hope to find in our spouse. This list is perfectly fine to make, but I think it is important to note the flexibility of this list. These wants should simply be viewed as "compromisable" desires; nothing more and nothing less. They are characteristics we would love for our spouse to possess, but they aren't of significant importance if they do not. In other words, they aren't deal breakers.

Needs, on the other hand, are "inflexible" desires, which aren't up for negotiation or compromise. These are the deal breakers. For instance, I want a woman who has been blessed with beautiful feet, but if you saw my last girlfriend's feet, you will understand how flexible and compromising I was with that characteristic. The looks of her feet weren't deal breakers, although they were very close. I do, however, need a woman who isn't allergic to telling the truth and treasures both giving and receiving honesty.

Honesty was the characteristic she lacked, hence her being referred to as my ex-girlfriend. At the end of the day, the looks of feet will not sustain me in a relationship, but someone who is and appreciates honesty just may. I've stated from the very beginning of this book that the way we have been taught to love and endure love is incorrect. My view is supported by statistics and the overwhelming amount of failed or failing relationships, versus the successful ones, including the ones you are personally aware of. I ask that you please keep an open mind to the sensibility of the ideology I will now expound on.

Life is not sustainable for long periods of time without three things: water, food and air. It's not like you can say, "I'll just take some food and water please, and you can hold the air; don't worry about me, I'll be just fine without it." Or, "Just give me some air and water, and you can keep the food, I don't really need to eat." Any combination you conjure up, missing just one of these three components, will inevitably end your life. The same concept is applicable to sustaining the life of a healthy, functional, monogamous relationship. If you have 10 characteristics in your needs column and you meet someone who provides an impressive nine out of the 10, then that person is not for you.

I know that statement will sound ridiculous to some people, and your initial reaction is to reject this belief. It is a difficult notion to ingest, because it has been embedded into our minds that we will never find the person who possesses everything on our "list." The first thing that commonly runs through people's minds when they hear this is, "No one is perfect!" This statement is absolutely true. No one is perfect, but there is someone out there who is specifically perfect for you. The question is are you willing to wait to meet that person, or are you willing to settle for someone who provides less than what you need from a spouse.

Understanding the difference between what you want and what you need from your spouse is paramount to knowing when to stay with or when to run from someone you are interested in romantically. Simply put, the perfect person for you isn't one without flaws, but rather one whose flaws are perfect for you and vice versa. Wants and needs are commonly conflated, but they are significantly different. Just as you would physically die if you are missing one of the three elements you need to live, your relationship will meet the same demise if your potential spouse is missing just one of the elements it needs to survive. The concept is exactly the same.

Let's create a scenario to further illustrate how important it is to not compromise anything listed in your needs column. I will list only five of the most popular characteristics people typically need to receive from their spouse in order to be happy, monogamous and functional. Many people say that honesty, fidelity, satisfying sex, effective communication and financial stability are at the top of their list. Now, let's suppose you've met someone who epitomizes whatever your definition of the perfect physical specimen is and more. Not only that, but also 20 million self-made dollars sit in this person's bank account, which is indicative of their intelligence, independence and entrepreneurial spirit. You've never met anyone more caring, affectionate, supportive, funny, fun and family oriented. But, unfortunately, the flaw they have is one that is extremely important to you, as it is to most other relationships ... sex!

You have not been pleased sexually by this person since you've begun being intimate, and it's not for the lack of effort. This person simply has no dexterity, coordination, rhythm, and no sexual understanding of how your anatomy works or how to effectively stimulate it. You have repeatedly explained your likes and dislikes, drawn maps, complete with stars and arrows, and still you're dissatisfied sexually. You've even sought the advice of sex therapists and still nothing has come close to resembling sexual pleasures for you. What do you do? You've been patient, prayed about it, communicated effectively about it, sought professional help about it, and it is still "not working."

Do you honestly believe you can maintain a happy, functional, monogamous relationship with this person for the rest of your life? If good, fulfilling sex is something you NEED to have in your relationship, then you cannot realistically be with this person, even with the other "perfect" attributes they have to offer. Eventually, the happiness, monogamy, or functionality will die, because fulfilling that vacancy, whatever it may be, MUST be filled. Remember, it is very possible to entertain a relationship and not be functional, monogamous or happy. It's done every single day! But, if your objective is to be all three of these things, then your needs can't be compromised. Having this mind-set should not be considered being picky, selfish or quitting. You are simply following the laws of nature and doing anything different is abnormal.

As previously stated, wants are desires that are compromisable, and needs are inflexible desires that aren't. That's the distinction between the two. Remember, we need water, food and air to sustain physical life. Now, we may WANT to eat a sirloin steak, wash it down with our favorite wine, while inhaling the purest air in the Maldive Islands, but these specific foods are not what we NEED to stay alive. You have your food, liquid and oxygen, but all three of these wants are negotiable and can be interchanged with other wants, e.g. eating lobster, drinking a tropical fruit punch, while inhaling and exhaling the air in India. This example is to illustrate the flexibility of our wants, and the inflexibility of what we need to live – food, water and air.

There are people who are very aware of what they need from their spouse and have the patience and strength to live their lives happily until they meet that special individual, and are sometimes labeled as being "too picky." A good friend of mine was dating a beautiful woman for a few years and they apparently got along very well. They had a great rapport, they shared many things in common and they were both at points in their lives where they were ready to settle down with one person for the rest of their lives. He and I were talking one day and I asked him when he was planning on marrying her. Without hesitation he replied, "Never!" I giggled a bit, because I thought he was joking. After realizing he was serious, I asked why he wouldn't marry her. He said because she was short. Again I giggled, but he was very serious and adamant about it.

Initially, I judged his reasoning and considered him to be ridiculously picky. He went on to say that he has a profound attraction for tall women, and he needs to be with someone who is 5'11" and taller and his girlfriend was only 5'2" on a good day. He said he would never feel fulfilled being with someone on the shorter side, and although his girlfriend was great, her height or lack thereof bothered him. I paused for a moment and really listened and processed what he was telling me. I understood it. Height was his NEED. I initially thought it was silly because height isn't a need of mine, when it comes to a characteristic for my spouse to have. If she was 5'10 and ¾ and he didn't want to be with her because she isn't 5'11," I would define that as being "picky." But someone who loves tall women, for whatever reason, shouldn't be judged for his preference. Similarly, someone shouldn't be judged for needing someone who is fit versus unfit or vice versa. Our needs are unique to us and should be respected and not judged.

Please take a few moments to complete an exercise I have designed, specific to you. Take as much time as you need and think about what your non-negotiables are in a relationship, or the things you need to receive from your spouse.

Frank C. Johnson

Close your eyes, take a deep breath and think of the things you are certain would rob you of the happiness in your relationship. What are the things you refuse to accept or tolerate in a relationship? The range can stretch from physical/emotional abuse to infidelity to pure boredom. This is your list of deal breakers, not anyone else's, regardless of what anyone else may think of them.

On a blank sheet of paper, I would like for you to label it "Column B" at the very top. Under the Column B heading, I would like for you to numerically list all of the deal breakers you were able to think of. Once you have Column B completed, read it over and make sure that these are absolute deal breakers. Now, I'd like for you to create a Column A on a separate sheet of paper. But this time, I would like for you to list the characteristics you absolutely NEED to find in your significant other. Remember, NEEDS are inflexible desires, not to be confused with wants, which are flexible and negotiable.

Close your eyes and think of things you know you CANNOT do without in your relationship. Your needs can range from physical traits, to emotional support to financial stability. Regardless of how silly or superficial you or anyone else may think of them, if you NEED it, right it down. Once you have created Column A, please reread it and make sure these are characteristics of someone who would potentially be the perfect person for you.

Now once you're sure that you've completed both Columns A and B, I'd like for you to complete one last task to complete the exercise. I would like for you to simply transfer just one of the characteristics from Column B to the very bottom of Column A. Then go back to the top of Column A and read the list again from top to bottom, including the last entry from Column B, and ask yourself, "Can I be happy, functional and monogamous with someone who possess every characteristic in this column?" You will find that after you've gotten to the very last characteristic at the bottom of your list, your answer will be a resounding, NO!

You can repeat that last step and interchange the last entry with any entered number from Column B to Column A, and you will still receive a no answer. You see, it doesn't matter if you've listed 50 needs in Column A, having just one intolerable, non-negotiable characteristic from Column B negates everything else. Some people may want to dispute this belief and say that one imperfection shouldn't be a strong enough reason to not pursue or to end a relationship, when there are so many other good characteristics being offered.

For those people who believe this, I ask, how many deal breakers do you need to accept before they actually become deal breakers? How much time should be spent unhappily before you decide that enough is enough and it's finally time to live the one life you have as happily as possible? I am not suggesting that you to run at the first sign of trouble or after a disagreement. Nor am I saying that you and your spouse will always be of one accord, without experiencing trying situations. But I am suggesting if you and your spouse have done the work of getting to learn about yourselves and you know how to differentiate between your wants and needs, getting through those tough times will be much more successful with the tools you have in your arsenal. If your needs are not being met, and you can discuss this with your spouse, it can then be determined if providing you with what you need is a possibility or not. If it isn't, then a decision of staying together or not can be made, since you now have the concrete information you need to make it.

Statistics, our own personal relationship history, and those of our family and friends support this fact. Fighting this notion will not make it any less true, regardless of how much you would like for it to be. If I hold something in the air and release it, I assure you it will come crashing down to the ground, as long as the laws of gravity are applicable. Regardless of how much I don't want it to fall, it is guaranteed to hit the ground. I can squint my eyes real hard, concentrate with tremendous fervor and might and will for it to levitate, but it won't. The object will still fall.

Satisfying our needs is analogous to the falling object. It's a law of nature. Self-preservation is an innate, natural instinct, and when our needs are not being met or satisfied, there will be a negative effect from it. Just as the object will crash and break, so will various aspects of our lives if we aren't being fulfilled. If we don't receive water, food or air, there will be a negative effect. If we don't receive support, fidelity, satisfying sex, effective communication or whatever else it is that we need in our relationship, there will be a negative effect. Again, no matter how hard you squint your eyes and concentrate with all your fervor and might, if you are not receiving your needs from your spouse or providing the needs for your spouse, I guarantee you will have an unhappy union. It's just the law. Check the stats and you will find that anyone who has had or is having a failed relationship, I guarantee you they are not receiving something they need from their significant other. We all have the capability to change this, but this will call for us to do things very differently. If we want different results, we have to have different actions.

I've discovered that relationships are very easy. It is actually the people who are difficult. People have the propensity to make simple things unnecessarily difficult, and that's mainly because we usually do what we want to do, rather than doing what we should do. I say again, we usually do what we want to do, rather than doing what we should do. I'm sure you can recall this type of behavior from your early childhood into present day.

As kids, we may have wanted to watch TV, instead of doing our homework or coming home after our set curfew time. If there were a law enforcer, as the universe enforces laws like gravity, you would have suffered a consequence.

84

Think about it for a moment. If WE ALL did what we are supposed to do, as it pertains to playing our part when it comes to relationships, we would never have any problems. But, that's not the reality, because people tend to do what they want to do, versus doing what they should do. I understand that we are not infallible beings, and at times will make poor choices. We may even suffer the consequences of those decisions, but if we were to try our best to be cognizant of other people's feelings, and how our choices can negatively impact other people, I believe we will do a much better job of making the right choice, versus the choice of self-gratification.

Just imagine, for a moment, if I could snap my fingers and everyone adopted my ideology on how to pursue and endure relationships, and they only entertained people who fulfilled their needs, without possessing any of their deal-breaking characteristics. The benefits would be tremendous. The divorce rate would decrease dramatically, there would be a lot less people involved in dysfunctional relationships, which automatically translates into there being a lot more single and available people to meet. Ultimately, this means there is a greater chance of meeting the right person for them, as they will not be tied up in a relationship that's not ideal for them. There would be a lot less people "trying to make it work" and a lot more grounded, self-aware single folks who are mentally and emotionally prepared to patiently wait to meet the "right" person who best compliments them. This is certainly the end goal, but in order to achieve it, there will have to be a mind shift from doing what has been customarily done to trying something different.

As previously stated, if most people adopted this ideology, there will inevitably be a lot more single people, because they wouldn't be involved in relationships that don't best suit them. This fact is what I find many people are most resistant to, because of their fear of being alone (Refer to Chapter 6). This fear is partially why so many people settle for someone who isn't ideal for them and end up being a part of the 80 percent of failed or failing relationships. It's time to face reality and adjust accordingly, so you can finally enjoy the benefits of true, healthy love.

Here is what's so interesting about my ideology and philosophy regarding the pursuit of happy, functional and monogamous relationships. Let's pretend everyone adopts my philosophy on relationships and puts everything we have discussed into action. The world we live in would barely be recognizable. Firstly, there would be a tremendous amount of people walking around with a renewed self-confidence and inner strength. They would have worked on and addressed whatever it was from their pasts that had caused their dysfunctional behaviors and weaknesses. They would inevitably be drawn closer to their life's purpose, because within the process of regression to heal whatever wounds stem from their pasts, they will become more introspective and will learn who they truly are. They will become more attuned with their spirit, their core, and their essence. This is when they will become the best version of themselves, and now they will be ready to meet someone who has gone through the same process and has become the best version of themselves, which is what everyone deserve to have.

In a nut shell, I believe this is the formula to having a happy, functional, monogamous relationship. Love of self and knowledge of worth. But this process just keeps on giving, because aside from you having a dream-filled, romantic relationship, this process positively impacts any relationship you have. When you are the best version of yourself, you can and will have a better relationship with your mother, father, sister, brother, friends, coworkers, or even perfect strangers. You will handle anger differently, conflict and drama will have no significance in your life; insecurities, and self-sabotaging vices will be of the past. Wouldn't it be great if I could just snap my fingers and make this happen? My dream is that everyone would adopt this philosophy, and there would be an incredible amount of newly single people, who no longer allow themselves to be a part of any unhappy, dysfunctional relationships.

Unfortunately, the reality is I cannot snap my fingers and have everyone adopt my philosophy and ideology on relationships, so instead I've written this book with the hope of people having a guide on how to achieve and enjoy the greatest gift ever given to us, true love. The title of this book is absolutely literal. My objective is to revolutionize how we love each other and the only way for that to happen is for us to effectively love ourselves. When we can love ourselves from the core outward, we will love others in ways you may not be able to fathom right now.

In closing, I pray that you will find a way to muster up the courage and strength necessary to remove any denial that has stunted your growth for all of these years, and you are finally able to completely ACCEPT your dysfunctions, flaws, imperfections, negative characteristics or difficult aspects of your personality and recognize them in your reality. That's the only place you will be able to conquer them. So, let's do something different when it comes to love and relationships, so we will have a different result. Become the best version of yourself, and we all will absolutely Revolutionize How We Love!

About Frank C. Johnson

Frank C. Johnson is a father and grandfather, but most of all a self-proclaimed lover of love. To his friends and family he is best known for his candid personality, which they often turned to for relationship advice. Frank's unbiased, straight forward, yet humorous counseling, has not only helped save some relationships, but he also helped other couples realize that separating was also an option, after agreeing they weren't the perfect match for each other. He has been featured on the podcast show, Crown Jewels on www.bboxradio.com and was also a featured speaker at the Glam Room, hosted by @Enjoilux.

Along with his first published book, Frank begins his journey to helping many more people to find true love and joy, with or without a partner.

For more information on Frank C. Johnson and his books, upcoming events and for booking speaking engagements, visit www.frankcjohnson.com and follow him on Instagram @frankcjohnson.